THINGS TO KNOW ABOUT SELF-LOVE

30 DAY AFFIRMATION GUIDE

A 30 Day Guide to help you stand strong against doubt, life pressures, and facilitate in loving yourself more. You are amazing. Start believing the truth of your greatness today.

BY ETTA ARLENE

Copyright © 2019 ETTA ARLENE
All Rights Reserved

DEDICATED TO YOU

Note From the Authors

Our main mission is to inspire people with our work and help people feel good about themselves. We want everyone to start to love who they are and be happy. We want you to let go of societal pressures that tell you who you are and who you should be. You are the only one who is allowed to decide that.

Preface

Before we get started let's eliminate the notion that in order to love yourself you must first change who you are. You at the core are exactly who you are supposed to be. You do not need to change anything about yourself but instead, change your self-perception and your thinking around self-worth.

We are talking about loving who you are. Any improvements are to obtain a skill or quality you admire for yourself not to be someone else.

Though this may seem like a guide we are not giving you strict instructions as to how you are required to read it. These are merely suggestions but in the end, you have the power. This book isn't designed to tell you who you should be. All it aims to do is wake you up to knowing, feeling, and loving your full potential.

Things To Know About Self-Love - Etta Arlene

It is to prompt you to recognize the inner greatness you have been hiding. It is to encourage you to stop playing small. Everything begins with self-love. When you love yourself everything tends to fall into place. That's all you need to know. That's all you have to do.

Things To Know About Self-Love - Etta Arlene

Recommended Instructions:

You are not supposed to read this book in one sitting. Do not rush to get through this book. Instead, read one page a day. If you must read more, make sure you feel - do not just state the words that are scrawled across the page. Be consumed by what you are reading. Read it twice. Read it until you know it is your truth. Make it your mantra. Revisit what connects with you. Understand that everything we are saying in this book is correct. The purpose is by the end of the 30 days you will feel the same. Everything we have written is made for you. Our intentions are pure and you are meant to be loved.

In this moment, just for the moment -

Forget about the past
Don't worry about the future
Feel the now

Things To Know About Self-Love - Etta Arlene

DAY 1:
Make a list of **5** things you like about yourself. Less is OK. More is OK. It can be as simple as *"I like the way I make coffee"*

01 I choose to stop apologizing for being me.

Lets begin with removing the idea that you need to apologize for simply existing. Embrace what makes you happy, embrace what you love, embrace who you are - shamelessly.

DAY 2:
Make a list of what you want in life no matter how big or small.

02 I deserve all good things.

You 150% deserve to have a good life. Stop living and thinking conditionally.

DAY 3:
Make a list of things you are good at and things you want to learn.

03 I release self-doubt.

You are in fact amazing. Stop doubting yourself, downplaying your greatness, and playing small.

DAY 4:
Write down any regrets or mistakes you have been holding. Then forgive yourself & lovingly let it go.
Example: *"I regret not writing that letter. I forgive myself & lovingly let it go."*

04   I forgive myself.

Forgive yourself for past mistakes, missed opportunities, hurt, or whatever else you are holding on to. Be thankful for the lessons and NOW lovingly let it go.

DAY 5:
List out every reason why you are great.
Example: "I am a great listener"

05   I acknowledge my own self-worth.

You are the only one who has the power to determine your worth. Stop letting others decide it for you.

DAY 6:
Write nice things about yourself.
Example *"My smile is stunning."*

06 I release negative self-talk.

Speak to yourself the way you speak to those you love. The way you feel about yourself is how the world will perceive you.

DAY 7:
Think about why you are amazing. Write it down no matter how weird, funny, small, or mundane. Example: *"I am amazing at making pancakes."* or *"I am an amazing sister."*

07 I am amazing.

That's right. You said it.
You're amazing

DAY 8:
Make a list of qualities you admire about yourself.

08 I am radiant.

You are filled with an inner glow that you should let shine. Energy is contagious. Help others with that vibe.

DAY 9:
Make a list of everything you are thankful for no matter how big or small.

09 I have everything I need within.

You are already filled with infinite potential. You already have power and capacity to be, do, feel, and have whatever you want.

DAY 10:
Make a list of things you are good at and really hype up those abilities.
Example: *"I am really, really good at dancing. I'm amazing at it."*

10 I let go of negative thoughts and feelings about myself.

Again, how you feel about yourself dictates how the world perceives us. Our thoughts create our reality.

DAY 11:
Challenge:
1. Close your eyes & sit comfortably.
2. Clear your mind & focus on your breathing.
3. Ask a question to yourself that you would like answered.
4. Return to focusing on your breath.
5. Listen to your inner guidance for the answer.

11 I embrace my inner magic.

You're magic. Believe and you can do anything.

DAY 12:
Make a list of things you love to do, things that make you happy, and/or new things you have always wanted to do but you have been putting off. Start working on doing those things today.

12 I make myself a priority.

Taking care of yourself and your well-being is not selfish. Put yourself first every now and then.

DAY 13:
Self-care is so important. Do something for you today.

13 I don't need anyone to complete me. I complete myself.

You read that right. Other people are a piece of your life but they do not define you.

DAY 14:
Make a list of things that make you happy. This can be people, foods, places, activities, etc.

14   I am in full control of my happiness.

Yes, we know this is a heavy one. However, often happiness can be a matter of perception and who you are allowing to be in control. What are you focusing on? Are you always looking at the bad? Who are you permitting into your life? Are you doing things you love? Now, what can you do to change this?

DAY 15:
Challenge:
Look in a mirror and tell yourself "I love you".

15

I am loved.

You are loved in ways you don't even realize. There is unconditional love in this universe. You are here for a reason. We love you. But, when you love yourself that's all you need.

DAY 16:
Do something today that stimulates the mind. (Feel free to draw or creatively write on this page)

16 My mind is brilliant.

Our brains are amazing and everyone has the power to think, dream, and feel. We were born with these epic super computers that we all just take for granted.

DAY 17:
Challenge:
Pick a day and only do the things you truly want to do. Speak honestly and say "no" when required. If it doesn't serve your greater good or make you happy, don't do it.

17 I am focused on being true to myself.

When you are true to yourself you do things that make you happy. When you are true to yourself you start to love your life and love who you are.

DAY 18:
Make a list of things you love about yourself.

18 I am loving who I am.

Love, love, love, love, love, love, love, yourself. Now. Right now.

DAY 19:
Create a list of things that make you happy.

19 I am committed to endless happiness.

Seek out happiness. Don't be afraid to do the things that resonate with you. Do things you enjoy doing. Separate from people and situations that do not bring you joy. Fight for your happiness.

DAY 20:
Make a list of **5** negative things you have thought about yourself. Turn those into positive statements. Commit to ending self-judgement today.

20 I release the need to judge myself and my body.

Stop comparing yourself to other people. We were created with our own unique beauty, minds, and talents. Embrace it.

DAY 21:
Make a list of challenges you have overcome no matter how big or small.

21

I am strong.

You've made it this far. You have the strength to get through anything.

DAY 22:
Make a list of things you like about yourself.

22 I am beautiful.

There is no one in the world like you.

DAY 23:
List off things about yourself that you are grateful for.

23 I believe in me.

Believe in your inner power. Trust your inner wisdom. How can you expect other people to believe in you if you don't believe in yourself?

DAY 24:
Make a list of goals you would like to achieve.

24. I am letting go of my worries, only focusing on self-improvement, self-love, and happiness.

Focus on your inner growth and experience on this earth. By worrying, you are not living in the present. If you don't take control of the present, you will have no control of your future.

DAY 25:
Challenge: We allow people and situations to affect us. You can decide what you permit into your life. You can have control over how you view yourself. Today refuse to let any person or situation make you feel like you are not worthy.

25 My thoughts and opinions matter. I matter.

No matter how small you think you are, you are here for a reason. We impact people in ways that we don't even know on a day to day basis. You are important. You are worthy. You matter.

DAY 26:
Challenge: Fully ignore the judgement of others, knowing the only approval you need is from yourself.

26

I approve of myself.

Seeking the approval from external sources is not sustainable nor is it empowering. If you approve of yourself, it wont matter what other people think. You will do things for your greatest good and drastically improve your mood, relationships, job, and quality of life.

DAY 27:
What makes you unique?

27 I embrace my uniqueness.

There is absolutely no one like you in this world. You are one of a kind. You are special. You are meant to be here. Know it, feel it, & embrace it.

DAY 28:
Make a gratitude list.

28 There is so much good in me.

Despite what other people say or how you may feel you are a good person. Your mistakes do not define you.

DAY 29:
Challenge: Today know and embrace your power. Go through the day knowing you are in full control.

29   I am recognizing and embracing my power.

Sometimes the external work can make us feel small and useless. But know we ALL have the power to change our lives and have a positive impact on the world. Own your inner power. Be in control of who you are and where you are going. All the power you seek comes from within.

DAY 30:
Make a list of why you love yourself and all of the things you love about yourself. (If this is hard to do - start over)

30

I love who I was.
I love who I am currently.
I love who I will be.
I love me.

Now that the 30 days are over our intention is that you have learned to love yourself more. Make these affirmations life principals knowing that they are true. These principals are not over now that you have completed the 30 days. Re-read this book as often as you want. Use any of the affirmations as needed. Pick any of the affirmations that have stood out to you and make it your daily mantra. Even when things get hard it is important to remember who you are, a awesome, beautiful human, meant to be here,
meant to radiate love.

About the Authors

Etta & Arlene are sisters who strive to make people feel good about themselves. In a world that is constantly telling people they are not good enough, they want to be a voice that says "Actually you are." Etta & Arlene are both Usui Reiki Masters and certified in Guided Meditation. Mindfulness is life. They have a blog that posts reiki, meditation, and mindfulness content.

www.ettaarlene.com

Made in the USA
Columbia, SC
06 October 2024